WP 10 9 8 7 6 5

78-0-7407-6852-1
-7407-6852-2

 Congress Control Number: 2007921932

y Creatif
ikit.com
ewsmcmeel.com

N: SCHOOLS AND BUSINESSES
McMeel books are available at quantity discounts with
ase for educational, business, or sales promotional use. For
, please write to: Special Sales Department, Andrews McMeel
LLC, 1130 Walnut Street, Kansas City, MO 64106.

One H
Chic

One Ho
Printed
any man
of repri
McMeel
Walnut S

09 10 11

ISBN-13:
ISBN-10:

Library

Licensed

www.co
www.an

ATTENT
Andrew.
bulk pur
informat
Publishin

One Hot Chick

In Search of Mr. Right ^Now

Cheryl Caldwell

a Co-edikit® book

**Andrews McMeel
Publishing, LLC**

Kansas City

So you feel like all of your friends
are merrily coupled . . .

Don't
Bother Me . . .

I'm Living
Happily Ever
After

and you keep attracting the wrong kind of people.

What am I?

FLYPAPER
for freaks!?!

Everyone seems to be luckier in love than you.

I had a
boyfriend,

but the clowns
ate him.

People tell you you're too picky.

I'm sorry, but I was looking for someone a little higher up (on the food chain).

But you're just putting your foot down.

If you don't
leave me,

I'll find
someone who will.

They tell you to put yourself out there.

Play
or be played.

But you've dated plenty.

So Many Freaks . . .

So Few Circuses

You just haven't found the right connection.

It sounds like English . . .

but I can't understand a word you're saying.

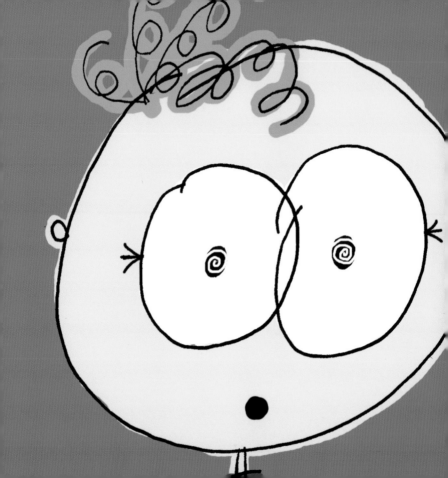

Or they weren't exactly mental giants . . .

We're all here . . .

because
we're not all there.

and you are.

I think . . .

therefore
I'm single.

If you happen to find someone
who sees things the way you do . . .

then they don't live up to your family's expectations.

Your trailer park called.

Their trash is missing.

And so it's back to the old drawing board.

I
want
my
fairy
godmother!

You spend hours trying to better yourself.

"Does this saddle make my butt look big?"

You hone your many qualities.

Sarcasm . . .

just one more
service
I offer.

You develop new hobbies.

Wanna play
a round?

Support
Your Local
Hooker

Your friends set you up with the "perfect match."

Nice

personality.

Does it come with
batteries?

Which leads you to continue trying on your own.

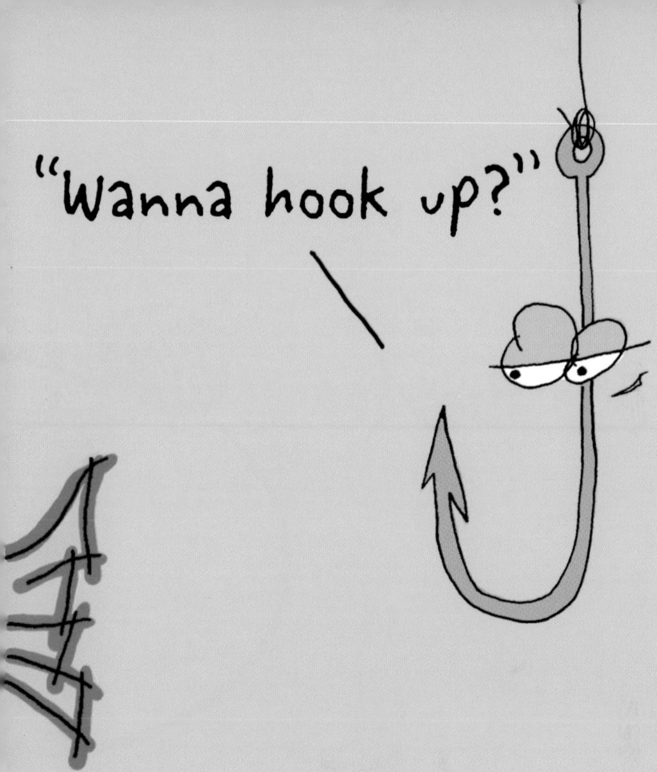
"Wanna hook up?"

Some say men are all dogs . . .

"Hey, baby! Show me your ticks!"

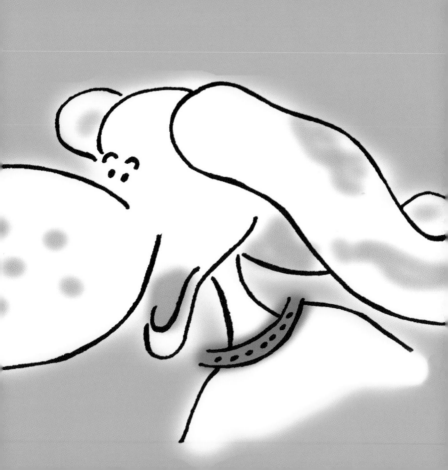

and girls are too catty.

Dogs have masters.

Cats have STAFF!

They are quick to point out how we are different . . .

when boys think, their brains explode.

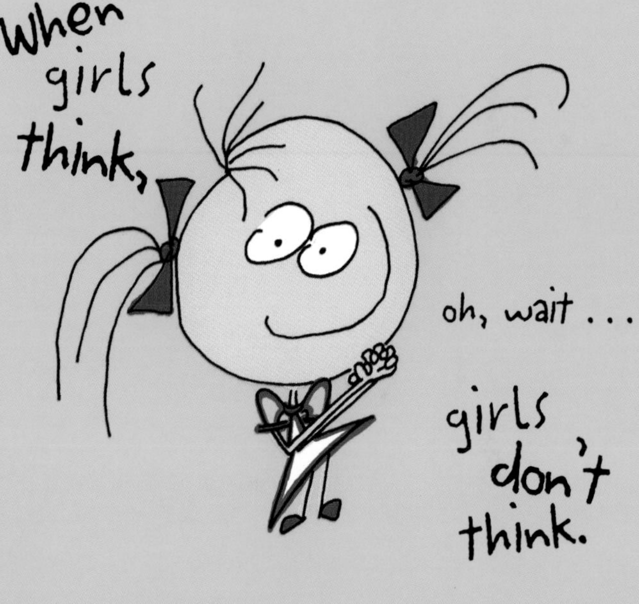
When girls think,
oh, wait . . .
girls don't think.

without ever celebrating our similarities.

You've tried everything.

I would not,
could not,
with a goat.

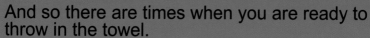

And so there are times when you are ready to throw in the towel.

But don't give up.

Tulips
are
better
than
one.

Give people a chance.

How sweet!
You think I care!

Don't limit yourself.

Hey, baby,
what's your
type?

Be willing to give a little.

How about a nice
tall glass of
never-gonna-happen?

Change your routine.

Nobody's
UGLY
after 2 a.m.

Get rid of old baggage.

Better
to have
loved and lost . . .

than to have spent
the rest of your life
with that psycho!

Mr. Right . . .

Mr. Right Now . . .

Mr. Right . . .

It will be worth the wait.

I consider
"on time"
to be when I get
there.

Let them know you're worth it . . .

You can't
afford me.

and so are they.

I'm so
miserable
without you . . .

it's almost like
you're still here.

Remember they're all princes . . .

You have to kiss
a lot of frogs . . .

(That's all.
You just have
to kiss a lot of frogs.)